NOTHING LACKING

MINISTER SANDRA BLACK

 Published in the United States of America by Gospel 4 U Network's Publishing department

ISBN – 978-0-9984665-3-8

Library of Congress Number – 2017904959

Printed in United States of America

April 2017

Content

Foreword

Minister Sandra Black is the founder of BCOC prayer-line ministry. She is a visionary leader and for the past 25 years, her life's mission is to bring awareness to the body of Christ. She speaks truth and honestly shares her experiences. She is truly a woman called by God to encourage and bring deliverance to His people. In 1997 I was lead to the Lord by Sandra and I'm proud to call her Spiritual mother and friend. Her tenacious spirit was evident as she shared her reasons for loving the Lord with me. My conversion was slow however, I never felt rushed, always felt loved and she never gave up or showed anger or frustration.

As you read this riveting memoir of abuse, pain, betrayal and ultimate forgiveness you too will understand why she believes "nothing lacking" through Christ Jesus and you won't be able to put this awesome, amazing book down!

-Minister Shelly Craig

Abundant Life Ministries

Wilmington

Acknowledgement

Thanking God for His Grace and Mercies! At that time when my mind was flickering, he was always there with me. To Shelly Craig, Mary Mark and aunt Stephanie Green. Words fail to provide adequate thanks for your constant abundant encouragement at all times, and your emotional and spiritual support, special thanks.

To my mother in Christ Rosiann Williams

Thank you for believing in me even when I wanted to stone myself, thanks for your patience and love towards me.

To Natalie Anderson

I will always be grateful for your sacrifices as you labored alongside me and the others, thanks.

Following Jesus is a journey that God didn't intended for us to walk alone.

To my Prayer line family, I am so thankful for your grace and patience. When I didn't deserve it, you diligently interceded on my behalf.

YOUR LOVE MEANS SO MUCH TO ME.

My Gratitude Is Endless.

-Minister Sandra Black

Dedication

This book is dedicated to my six children Roxanne, Katon, Kamozue, Davodo, Karen and Gabriella, also to my eight grandchildren, who are the earthly lights of my life.

This book is also dedicated to all the men and women of God who suffered and who are still suffering in silence as they go through this journey called life.

I speak for you!

Introduction

We are traveling a path of life where there is danger lurking everywhere, but before we were born God already predestined our lives. The road to wholeness comes with a price because it's the process leading towards greatness.

Made in God's image as a child of sovereign love, there is a war going on between light and darkness, and in this war, it is all about who will win. The scars are so deep that now and then it closes and opens. The mantle of shame covers so tightly that when we try to get away, we stumble. To slay the giants and conquer the city, the walls of shame, fear, and worm mentality must be dealt with.

Nothing Lacking! Take off the mask and open the door. Shout freedom! The eyes of your understanding are enlightened that you will know the hope of His calling. Put your past into perspective and change your focus. If you're continually looking behind, you cannot see where you're going.

God can take a dried up, useless life and transform it into a life of purpose and grace. He is able to change desert areas of our lives into fields of blessing and abundance. The cross is the demonstration of Nothing Lacking, for in Christ dwelleth all the fullness of the God Head. We are complete in Him.

A word about the depth of this book: It is written so that as many people as possible can benefit from it. Get ready to walk in the fullness of your blessing.

NOTHING LACKING!

NOTHING LACKING

James 1:4 ~ Let perseverance finish its work so that you may be mature and complete, not lacking anything.

CHAPTER 1

LIGHT IN A DARK ROOM

One day, a rich man threw a Best Smile Pageant. It consisted of ten women. Nine of these women were professional models and had the nicest clothes, the most expensive shoes, the best makeup and the sort. The tenth woman was there almost by accident. The rich man perused the contestants and as he walked pass the first nine woman he told them all things like "Very nice", "Looking good", and "Great smile". Once he got to the tenth woman he stopped and looked at her deeply in her eyes and said "Exquisite, simply beautiful".

The first nine woman had been trained professionally and knew exactly what to do in these kind of contests and all of them were extremely confident. The tenth woman was a normal woman, whose lights had been turned out the night before, and who could barely take care of her child because of very hard times, she had been entered by her friend.

The rich man said if you think you've won step forward. The first nine women stepped forward, the tenth woman stayed back. The rich man said, if you stepped forward I thank you for entering but neither of you have won. He then said to the tenth women, "Will you please step forward?" She stepped forward. He declared to everyone there that the tenth woman was the winner to everyone's amazement because she had on normal clothes, and average makeup, and spruced up shoes. He was asked later, how did he come to his conclusion that this woman had the best smile. He replied that "The prettiest smile is the one that is produced in spite of negative circumstances." He went on to explain "The other women were very beautiful but they didn't have any light within them because it could clearly be seen that they expected to be chosen. The tenth woman was the only light in a dark room and her ability to smile and be radiant in spite of her circumstances was the most beautiful thing I've seen in a long time."

I, at one point in my life, was a lot like the tenth woman. Smiling in spite of all of my life circumstances. Putting on my best face even though I was in lack in the natural and in the spiritual. I had mastered the art of pressing on even when I was an inch from giving up.

One of the most common reasons for a person to give up on their marriage, business relationship, faith, and/or even life is the fact that there is an inadequacy of contentment that leads to resentment and a feeling of lacking. This feeling whether real or perceived is one of the biggest reasons of giving up and can lead to premature decision making and giving up on your hopes, dreams, and purpose. My life has taught me the danger of this condition and God has led me to tell everyone that you don't have to live like this because God wants us all to be complete and whole; nothing lacking, nothing missing, and nothing broken.

The opposite of nothing lacking is being in lack, need, and want. And this is counter to what we know that God wants for our lives. God told us that He wishes above all that we would be prosperous and in good health.

3 John 1:2

Beloved, I ***wish above all*** *things that thou mayest prosper and be in health, even as thy soul prospereth.*

When we're living in the spirit of the aforementioned scripture and can truly say that we are prospering in our spirituality, in our mentality, in our personal relationships, and in our public life; then we can truly say that we are truly living according to the wish or will of God. Remember, the scripture says, "I wish" which means that it is God's will for you man of God and woman of God to live an abundant life.

There is no better feeling than when you know you don't owe anybody or any entity anything and this in essence is what it means to be totally free of lack as we travail through this human experience. To live in the will of God means that you have an abundance of faith which leads to a perfect peace, knowing that ***all*** *things shall work together for your good*; as it says in Romans 8:28.

If I can be honest, this is the part of my life where I, at one time, struggled. I went through a very trying time in my life with feeling as if something was missing. I knew that my salvation was sure but there was no fruit, or, no good fruit. I would ask myself, "Where is my joy? My peace? How can I be healed? When am, I going to be healed?" Like that woman bent over for 18 years in Luke 13, my whole life was bent over. And I thought that I'd never again stand straight.

In my dark room, where I put my furniture behind the door to keep me from my inner self, I would ask will the light shine? Will I see the light of release? My heart cried out loud for deliverance but no one heard me because the cry was on the inside. Some of you reading this right now can relate to what I went through and some of you are going through this right now.

So, I made up in my mind that I needed to climb out of this pit. First, I started renewing my mind by not only hearing but believing God's word. And God allowed me to see one day that I am in Christ Jesus. And if I am in Christ Jesus, I can have everything that He has and be everything that He is and live a glorious life in Him. God explained to me **Ephesians 2:10 (AMP)**; *10 For we are His workmanship [His own master work, a work of art], created in Christ Jesus [reborn from above—spiritually transformed, renewed, ready to be used] for good works, which God* *prepared [for us] beforehand [taking paths which He set], so that we would walk in them [living the good life which He prearranged and made ready for us].*

Basically, the Bible says that we have been created ***in*** Christ Jesus. Isn't that awesome? We were born from above to do good works of which God has already prepared for us to do. I don't know about you but that right there is a revelation that moves everything inside of me letting me know that this life was designed for us to win. It has been already ordained for us to prevail and figure it all out and we will as long as we keep Christ Jesus in the middle of it.

The other thing that we have to do is confront ourselves. When we know that our flesh and emotions have gotten out of line and we don't confront it, we're in sin.

James 4:17 (ESV) *So whoever knows the right thing to do and fails to do it, for him it is sin.*

I confronted myself. I demanded of myself to no more hide behind the mask. I decided that I would no longer succumb to fear. I locked the door and threw away the key. So I surrendered myself. No more living a lie, wearing a mask. I realized that I did in fact, have the power to change. But first, I had to put the past into perspective. All the demons that apprehended me, I released knowing that I can live. I must live.

But first, I had to die to self. I had to die to all of my own carnal desires. I had to die to all of my wayward ways, and selfish ambitions. My "self" had to die. Not that I was physically doing something wrong, but I was in the prison of my own mind which kept rehearsing all of the evil things that I had to endure in my life. For instance, my struggle to survive molestation, physical, verbal, and sexual abuse. I kept rehearsing my abuse. Which led me down to a path of depression and negativity that almost made me end my life, simply to feel no more pain.

Pain is a good indicator that something is not normal or that something is wrong. However when you rehearse your pain it becomes a platform for pity. Self-pity to be exact. And self-pity leads to bitterness. Die to self-pity beloved. Die to sin.

Satan is an accuser of the brethren and I've learned that one of his very real tactics is to never let you live down anything you've done, that was remotely ungodly. He'll bring up every error that you've ever done because he knows that the sins that you committed in the past are the same ones that you will commit in the future. Why is this true you may ask? Because God is immutable, meaning unchangeable. Which means for the most part, man, being made in God's image, does not change.

So I was determined to die so I can live. I realized that there is no perfection in me but I am perfect because of my eternal union with the infinitely perfect Christ. This perfection is absolute and unchangeable. And it is this perfect relationship that guarantees that I will be made whole. Chronic guilt, apathy, depression, failure, constant desire for approval; no more! I receive my joy. I receive my thankfulness to God. Love and peace flood my soul. Oh, did I forget to mention forgiveness? Yes, forgiveness. I slayed my giants. The fact is, it is impossible to live victoriously without slaying your giants and being courageous. That bully called fear is no more!

So I rise and I shine light in the dark places. Beauty for my ashes. No more searching for shelter. God designed me to be a unique, distinct, significant person. Outward size and shape and features no more matter. But the real me, God developed. So I lack nothing. Nothing lacking.

God in me, behind and before is the whole me. My broken heart was healed. My sight was discovered. I was set free. My bruise, my wound…no more! No more shame. I am a vessel of honor. I am a lily among the thorns. But I am loved by God and me. I am committed to the process. And though it has not always been easy, there is nothing lacking. I am God's masterpiece. My future is bright. I found my song and I'm singing loud, walking tall. I am confident knowing that my life is but a weaving between God and me. I was trying to choose the color. But I was foolish, knowing that I am the underside. We will meet again on this journey call life.

Truly when the word of God says, "All things work together for the good to them that love God and were called according to his purpose." Until we truly understand what that really means, only then will we understand that in spite of what we are going through, in spite of our life situations, there is nothing lacking in Christ Jesus. And because we are in Him and He's in us, we are complete. Nothing lacking.

I like this word that says, "For ye are dead," in the book of Colossians.

Colossians 3:3
For ye are dead, and your life is hid with Christ in God.

So I encourage everyone today. I will no longer be fooled by the outer garment. Don't you allow yourselves to be fooled by the outer garment. I will no longer be fooled by the voices because I know that I am complete in Christ. I was conceived in love because God so loved the world that he gave His only begotten Son that whosoever believeth in Him will not perish. I was conceived in love and there is nothing lacking in that true love of God.

Now, one must understand that when you truly realize that you are loved by God, our Creator, a million times more than we could ever love ourselves or ever love another person it puts you into an abundance of God. And being in abundance leads to perfect peace. The Bible says this to us in Isaiah 26:3 where it says:

You will keep him in perfect peace, whose mind is stayed on you: because he trusts in you.

Peace is a covenant word and at its core it means that there is nothing lacking, nothing broken. The Hebrew word for peace is Shalom which is pronounced Shalom.

God is our Peace and He will grant you more peace as you continuously draw close to Him. Consider **Isaiah 26:3** 21st Century King James Version (KJ21)

3 Thou wilt keep him in perfect peace, whose mind is stayed on Thee, because he trusteth in Thee.

One of the attributes and names of God is Jehovah Shalom, meaning the God of Peace. This aspect of Jehovah's character was revealed to Gideon, in Judges 6:23-24, when God told Gideon that he would not die when there were people at war with his country. God told him that even though it looked like an unstable situation for the moment, he would have peace. The caveat to the instructions that God gave Gideon was that he would have to go to war with a minimum amount of people to get that peace. And sometimes our peace is dependent upon our willingness to fight for it.

When God gives us instructions we have to rehearse His instructions concerning us. The more we keep our mind on Him and His Word, the more perfected our peace becomes.

God told Gideon to go to battle with just a few hundred men, showing that God wanted share the victory with Gideon. See sometimes God is just trying to remove the unnecessary out of your life so that the necessary can help you win. When you start seeing people being plucked from your circle it's not that God is against you. It could actually mean that He is aligning and revealing those that have value. Could it be the people that you're crying about was taking away value from your life? Look at things from God's perspective, not yours.

Another part of the instructions showed that Gideon would not have to engage the enemy physically, showing that the battle wasn't really Gideon's it was the Lord's. Most of the time our battles are already fixed and all we have to do is walk this thing out and rely on God.

Only upon reliance upon Almighty God can we know His peace which will bring about triumph over all our enemies. Trust Him dear one that He will come through for you. I know it is easy to go along with the prevailing sentiments of our current day and worry, worry, worry. But worrying and fear is an offense to God because it means that we are doubting His abilities and doesn't show any difference between us and the world.

As believers in Christ Jesus we have to be careful not to compromise God's word to fit in with the world, because we are afraid of hurting someone feelings. Some of us are so overly concerned about what the world thinks of us, afraid of offending or being politically correct. Certainly, as believers in Christ, we are not to go out of our way to offend anyone personally, but the truth is that the Word of God itself is offensive because it's contrary to the world system. And the preaching of the Cross goes against living a sinful lifestyle because the Word tells us in **Matthew 16:24** *"24 Then Jesus told his disciples, "If anyone would come after me, let him deny himself and take up his cross and follow me."*

Equally offensive is the necessity of dying to self in order to follow Christ". The key word is deny. The world's system tells us to indulge in and do whatever we like if we are not hurting anyone. But in God's Kingdom we are too deny ourselves (flesh) and follow the example we have in Jesus Christ if we want to inherit the Kingdom of God. This is not always easy but we die daily to do so. Consider Paul's letter to the church of Corinth:

1 Corinthians 6:9–11 *"9) Or do you not know that the unrighteous will not inherit the kingdom of God? Do not be deceived: neither the sexually immoral, nor idolaters, nor adulterers, nor men who practice homosexuality, 10) nor thieves, nor the greedy, nor drunkards, nor revilers, nor swindlers will inherit the kingdom of God. 11) And such were some of you. But you were washed, you were sanctified, you were justified in the name of the Lord Jesus Christ and by the Spirit of our God."*

So even though your initial reaction to dying to yourself, which means dying to your flesh, may seem like a daunting task. After you read 1 Cor. 6:9-11 where it tells us that unrighteousness can't inherit the Kingdom of God; it puts our whole lives into perspective. We're not trying to live a life that is pleasing to God to please ourselves.

We're trying to obtain a level of living that is considered standard for being a citizen of God's heavenly kingdom. There will be no admission into God's holy city for sinners. That's enough motivation for me to die to my flesh and any earthly pleasure that God has not sanctioned. How about you dear one?

Remember it's not our words, it's God's word that convicts the world of sin. Our duty is to speak God's word in Love as God gives us the opportunity to witness to the unsaved; **1 Peter 3:15 ESV** says *"But in your hearts honor Christ the Lord as holy, always being prepared to make a defense to anyone who asks you for a reason for the hope that is in you; yet do it with gentleness and respect"*

So, our job is to take God at His word and understand that He is serious about holiness and Godly living for us and the world. Unholy living leads to lack and premature death because the wages of sin is death. So we have to be fervent in our effort to live lives that are honorable and pleasing in the sight of God. We also have to fervent in helping our family and friends to live these kind of lives as well The Bible say that we are to restore our brother and sister in Christ who are living sinful lifestyles cautiously and meekly, lest we fall as well. Consider **Galatians 6:1** *"Brethren, if a man be overtaken in a fault, ye which are spiritual, restore such an one in the spirit of meekness; considering thyself, lest thou also be tempted."*

The word of God was never meant to be comfortable; **Hebrews 4:12 (KJV)** *"12 For the word of God is quick, and powerful, and sharper than any two-edged sword, piercing even to the dividing asunder of soul and spirit, and of the joints and marrow, and is a discerner of the thoughts and intents of the heart."*

When you are not in lack it means that you are living in peace in many areas. Peace is a Covenant word, that at its Hebrew core means 'nothing broken, nothing missing'.

Another name and attribute of God is Jehovah Shalom, meaning the God of peace. Shalom, the Hebrew word for peace, typically is used to describe an absence of hostility or strife. Peace is the opposite of the rivalry, instability, and division brought by envy and ambition. So if you are full of envy and strife you are not and will never be completely whole and in perfect peace. Get rid of it. If you are full of internal and external conflict you are not and cannot be in perfect peace. Get rid of it. If you are competing with others to prove to yourself that your life has value you are in lack and void of God's perfect peace. Deal with this deficiency. Shalom indicates a total fulfillment that comes when individuals experience God's presence.

The key to our restoration is contained in God's peace. Because the truth is that Jesus is our peace. He is the final sacrifice and hence, has united us together in His peace. Ephesians 2:14-16 shows us that Jesus, also known as Yeshua, which is also translated as Yahoshua, who is Jehovah Shalom; is the final sacrifice.

Ephesians 2:14-16

14) For He is our peace, who hath made both one, and hath broken down the middle wall of partition between us,

15) having abolished in His flesh the enmity, even the law of commandments contained in ordinances, that He might make in Himself one new man out of the two, so making peace,

16) and that He might reconcile both unto God in one body by the cross, having slain the enmity thereby.

Lastly, regarding the subject of being complete in God's peace. Shalom is a greeting and a benediction. Which lets us know that everything that we need is contained in God's peace. When you say hello to God, He welcomes you into His peace. When you leave this life, He promises that to be absent from the body is to be present with the Lord.

Everything on the outside of Christ's peace will leave you wanting and lacking; a serious lesson that I had to learn the hard way. Entering into a state of wholeness and unity with God signifies restoration that come only come from the only one who has the power to restore. The shalom of God signifies a sense of well-being and harmony both within and without. It fosters health, happiness, quietness of soul, preservation, prosperity, tranquility, security, safety and includes everything that makes life worthwhile.

Shalom involves more than forgiveness of sin, in that living a full life, prosperity, and peace with humanity is the expected result of it.

Philippians 4:6-7 (KJV)

6) *Be careful for nothing; but in everything by prayer and supplication with thanksgiving let your requests be made known unto God.*

7) And the peace of God, which passeth all understanding, shall keep your hearts and minds through Christ Jesus.

CHAPTER 2

THE POWER OF THE TONGUE

Psalms 34:9-10 (KJV)

9 *O fear the* L*ORD, ye his saints: for there is no want to them that fear him.*

10 *The young lions do lack, and suffer hunger: but they that seek the* L*ORD shall not want any good thing.*

Declare and decree that because you seek the Lord, you lack no good thing. Say it one more time men and women of God, but this time make it personal. "Because I seek the Lord, I lack no good thing."

It may not feel like it right now, but it doesn't mean that it is not the case. We are the prophets of our lives and we are the products of what we think and then say. The more you confess the Word of God over your life, the more changes occur in the spirit realm. What if I told you that nothing happens in the natural realm until something first happens in the spirit realm? Well it's true. Nothing can happen to you or anyone else, for that matter, that God hasn't permitted.

Remember Job? Job's name was offered to the enemy to be buffeted by him. God allowed Lucifer to mess with Job's family and wellbeing. The only thing that he wasn't allowed to touch was Job's life. And so satan went to work and started messing with Job, his family, and his business.

I believe that God would've had to pick another candidate if Job knew to confess these scriptures over his life. Of course he didn't have Psalms chapter 34 at his disposal during his time, but I'm sure you get the point.

Proverbs 18:21 (KJV)

> *Death and life are in the power of the tongue: and they that love it shall eat the fruit thereof.*

So, our ability to decree and declare a thing according to God's Word is so important because we have established that we will have what we say because death and life are in the power of the tongue. Even though this is truth, it doesn't mean that we will not still have to go through some kind of storms in our lives.

As Christians we are all going through some type of storm, but we must continue to endure it no matter what. Each trial is part of the process that we have to go thru to get to the promise He has for us. We must not forsake the process and let patience have its perfect work.

James 1:4 says, *But let patience have its perfect work, that you may be perfect and complete, lacking nothing.*

It was going through this process that finally developed me to the point that I could boldly declare that I am a child of God. I am delivered. I am set free. I am a winner. I will win. I will no longer be fooled with the things around me because now I receive it that greater is He that is in me than he that is in the world. My mind is free. My spirit is free. And now I can really shout, "Freedom!"

As I recall, one day I was at my house and the voices in my head were just telling me, "Don't you realize you're going crazy? Go to the hospital and check yourself in." I got up and went to the hospital. I checked myself in. And as I was walking around and looking at all these people, I heard another voice say, "You don't belong here." Oh how my root was so on top. My root was way up, not inside. Oh how my root was not stabilized. My root was not strong because I was going through all this terror in the night and in the day.

My reference to my root is speaking to me not being grounded. A tree is only as strong as its roots. No matter how beautiful and big a tree looks, if it cannot withstand the strong winds of this earth realm it will not stand. The deeper the roots the more likely that the tree will survive. If the roots are implanted in shallow ground the tree will fall. If your roots come to the service or worse comes out of the ground the tree is doomed for destruction and is about to die. My roots were showing. They were way up and not stabilized.

I was just going through. I was walking around like a time bomb but looking for help, not even telling anyone I needed help. But I remember going to different churches, not because I wanted to go to them but because I believed I would find that particular somebody who was like Jesus. Somebody who could see that I was crouched over with an infirmity. Someone who can deliver me. Someone. Just someone. My God, my God. But then I realized when the mind is bending and the gale attacks within, it feels like every hope is gone.

What I know is it takes roots; deep roots in Christ Jesus to carry on. Shallow roots are for the fearful and uncommitted person that is resigned to losing anyway. It takes courage. It takes a militant mind to move forward. It takes getting up and claiming the Word of God and knowing that we can do it in the name of Jesus. So, you know, it just takes time. Deepen your roots so that they become powerful and deep.

After you develop strong, powerful, and deep roots, your next responsibility will be to keep them stabilized and fertilized. Roots become unstable and less fertile when your mind starts swaying. So, keeping your mind intact is critical because the enemy wants us to believe that the particular stronghold of being in lack, is normal.

The word strongholds is found once in the New Testament, used metaphorically by Paul in a description of the Christian's spiritual battle: *"3) For though we walk in the flesh, we do not war after the flesh. 4) For the weapons of our warfare are not carnal, but mighty through God to the pulling down of strong holds;"* **(2 Corinthians 10:3-4, KJV)**

It is the enemies job to steal, kill, or destroy and if he can't kill you, he will try to steal and destroy your joy. He does this by erecting strongholds in your mind, body, and even spirit. I cannot tell you how much time I have wasted in my life because of allowing myself to be trapped and stopped by strongholds. You might be asking why am I saying allowing myself to be trapped. The reason why I say that is because we are never really trapped unless we want to be or think that we are. The enemy makes mirages and erects illusions as if you're imprisoned when really you can walk out of that illusionary place anytime you want to beloved. Isn't that awesome?

I thought that I had been tainted because of the terrible things that had been done to me and that I had to endure. And it wasn't until I realized that I didn't have to live in that place of self-pity which later turned into bitterness that I was set free.

Do you know that we all deal with strongholds? And guess what? It is the strongholds in our lives that tries to hold on to us for the rest of our respective lives but we just have to believe that God is greater and walk right through these barriers. We are the ones who have the power. Dear ones, in our physical and mental being, it is we who have the power to either stay trapped or instead be set free. In our spiritual capacity, our freedom is based in Jesus Christ.

In **John 8:31** it says, 31) *To the Jews who had believed him, Jesus said, "If you hold to my teaching, you are really my disciples.* 32) *Then you will know the truth, and the truth will set you free."*

I decree, and declare, that for the one who is reading this book right now, that for you there is nothing lacking, nothing missing and nothing broken. Say these words with me dear one: I decree and declare that God will enlarge my territory and that no harm will come to me. I claim that whatever God has for me is for me. Whatever has been stolen from me is rightfully mine and I'm taking it back in Jesus' name. The cross gave me access, all provision has already been made and I'm walking in my God given authority. I am walking in faith and favor is mine.

Doesn't that feel good? You just took back what is rightfully yours. However, let's go back. The Holy Spirit helped me to realize that I was crawling like a worm. I was crawling around on my belly because I could not get free. I did not understand that when I present my body to God as a living sacrifice that my mind is supposed to be renewed. I had a fundamental misunderstanding. Part of that misunderstanding was that for my mind to be renewed I had to study and read the word of God and apply the word of God. Yes, I studied. Yes, I read. Yes, I preached. But was I truly applying the word of God? Because the Word of God wasn't manifesting inside of me as it should've because there was fear there that was blocking any tangible manifestation of the evidence of God's power in my life.

But one day I knew that I hit rock bottom. And when I hit rock bottom I realized that I had nowhere to go so I had to make rock bottom my foundation. Then I realized. Guess what? I am somebody. I am somebody. I was born to live. I was born for a purpose. I was born to be set free. I was born to make a difference. I was born to understand that greater is He that is in me than he that is in the world. I was born to know that God, when the fullness of time came, sent His son that I might be set free and who God sets free is free indeed. And that day when I understood that there is nothing lacking because God's word is true, was the biggest epiphany of my life. And the word of Isaiah chapter 40 came back and said, "Have you not known? Have you not heard?" And then I realized that yes, I know. Yes, I have heard. And I started to apply the word of God in and over my life. And then I was never the same again. This crouched over spirit, this dead person became alive that day. This wounded soul was able to be healed that day. This wounded soul was able to be set free that day, not only in words but in actions. I was able to take control of my life in Jesus Christ. I was able to understand what it said, "Now unto him that is able to keep me from falling." I realized that I cannot keep me but God kept me and will keep me. I realized I can go forward. I can fly high because nothing is lacking. I realized that there is nothing under the sun that I cannot accomplish because there's nothing lacking. I realized that I am seated in Christ in heavenly places even though simultaneously, I am supposed to take dominion in the earth until He comes. I finally understood that my job; or should I say our job; is to occupy until He comes. I realized that I was free. I am free. The prison was an illusion. The stronghold was a façade that remained because of my choice. Finally, I am free.

Someone reading this book right now is coming to the end of their storm. God wants you to read what He told the Hebrew Israelites when they were finally coming to the end of their time in the wilderness for forty years. Read this set of scriptures every morning for 31 days man or woman of God to program your spirit for your season of plenty in God.

Deuteronomy 8:6-14 (21st Century King James Version)

6) Therefore thou shalt keep the commandments of the Lord thy God to walk in His ways and to fear Him.

7) For the Lord thy God bringeth thee into a good land, a land of brooks of water, of fountains and depths that spring out of valleys and hills,

8) a land of wheat, and barley, and vines, and fig trees, and pomegranates, a land of olive oil, and honey,

9) a land wherein thou shalt eat bread without scarceness. Thou shalt not lack any thing in it; a land whose stones are iron and out of whose hills thou mayest dig brass.

10) When thou hast eaten and art full, then thou shalt bless the Lord thy God for the good land which He hath given thee.

11) "Beware that thou forget not the Lord thy God in not keeping His commandments and His judgments and His statutes which I command thee this day,

12) lest when thou hast eaten and art full, and hast built goodly houses and dwelt therein,

13) and when thy herds and thy flocks multiply, and thy silver and thy gold is multiplied, and all that thou hast is multiplied,

14) then thine heart be lifted up and thou forget the Lord thy God, who brought thee forth out of the land of Egypt, from the house of bondage,

CHAPTER 3

ESCAPING FROM PRISON

Galatians 5:17

Stand fast therefore in the liberty wherewith Christ hath made us free, and be not entangled again with the yoke of bondage.

Before I go any further in this body of work, I believe that you have to understand where I came from to appreciate where I have arrived and who I truly am. There is a reason why God has blessed me with the ability to reach back and help someone else. My completeness today came at a terrible price and after many seasons of being broken, lonely, and incomplete. The process that it took to get me to the woman that I am today was not easy but it was worth it. I am standing in God's liberty today only because God, in His infinite mercy and grace, made me free.

I did not get saved until the age of 16 and even then I was still struggling with living a Godly life. I struggled because of more than one thing, but one of my greatest hurdles was the fact that when I was but a young girl, I was molested. And because of the abuse enacted against me, I felt as if I was worthless and damaged to the point that it didn't matter what happened to me. I grew up with a small sense of self-worth because the enemy kept feeding my mind that this was happening to me because I was worthless and not special.

I am often pressed and even vexed in my spirit with the understanding that there are many women who have gone through what I've had to endure. To these women, I say, it was never your fault and don't you ever blame yourself for another person's sickness and mistakes. An abuser will abuse you and leave a spirit to make you think it was your fault that you were abused. Reject this foolishness and never accept this lie into your spirit because it will contaminate your soul.

A lot of times when we undergo a traumatic event or experience, damage occurs, and we don't even know it. For the sexual abused, many of us have to deal with self-worth issues because our innocence has been compromised, which can lead to horrid self-image issues. This is the case because when you're young you are under the impression that you are the most special little girl or little boy and then when that specialness is violated, it leaves you broken. Hence, a part of the reason why I grew up feeling broken.

To be honest, I believe that I was grown like many children are grown. With a naivete regarding the evils of the world. And because you possess the innocence of a child, and for the most part, never had to endure anything evil until you are approached by it, it's easy for a predator to come in and defile.

Notwithstanding what happened to me but from a young age I felt as if I was living in a dark place. I could never find myself nor did I ever feel as if I had a firm foundation because every time we would settle some where we had to get up and move again. I moved so many times as a young girl and I withdrew within myself more and more every time that we had to do it.

A victim of molestation I found myself going through many relationships and just being downright promiscuous, because I never felt good enough for anybody. I honestly looked at myself as damaged property. Why would anyone really want me? Can't they see that I am damaged? Can't they see that I am lacking something? To be honest I didn't even feel good enough for myself because I was locked in a prison and

I didn't know how to get out.

There was a fight going on within me and I was too immature to understand it. When I got older I ran upon a passage of scripture that explains this season of my life perfectly:

Romans 7:21-25

[21]So I find this law at work: Although I want to do good, evil is right there with me. [22]For in my inner being I delight in God's law; [23]but I see another law at work in me, waging war against the law of my mind and making me a prisoner of the law of sin at work within me. [24]What a wretched man I am! Who will rescue me from this body that is subject to death? [25]Thanks be to God, who delivers me through Jesus Christ our Lord! So then, I myself in my mind am a slave to God's law, but in my sinful natured a slave to the law of sin.

As I said, I got saved at the age of 16. My sixteenth year on this earth was a pivotal time in my life. It was in my sixteenth year on God's green earth that a gunman put a gun at my head and was about to pull the trigger, but God! I know that it was only the grace of God that spared my life because a week after that incident the same gunman pulled his gun on another 16 year old, but this time he pulled the trigger, and killed her. God was revealing to me way back then that my life had a purpose. He was letting me know that even though I had to endure a few things and would undoubtedly have to endure a few more things, He was there, protecting me, and He wasn't going to allow anything to take me out before my purpose is realized and He will not allow more on me than I could bear.

I was very promiscuous, due to low self-worth, but God covered me with His grace and He didn't allow me to be shamed via disease or otherwise, but I knew that if He had allowed any of those things, I deserved it. I was in a dark place and I didn't know how to get to the light.

As I maneuvered in this darkness I entered into the institution of marriage, but because of my incompleteness, my marriages failed. When you get married it's not 50/50 to make 100 it's 100/100 to make one. Because when the two enters into the covenant of marriage they become one.

Understand this, if you're not 100 percent at the point of saying, "I do", you're bringing a half of a person to an institution that takes two complete individuals. Word of advice don't even think about marriage if your plan is to give your spouse only 50 percent of yourself.

Because of these scenarios I struggled with my spirituality because even though I found out the truth, that God had a better way, and that way is Jesus, I couldn't break free from the stronghold of sin. What do you do when you're in the light yet the darkness is still all around you?

What am I saying? Even after all of these things, and I grew up, I was in the light of Christ, yet I was still hiding. One time I can remember very vividly, is after my daughter and I was secure in the house, I pushed a couch in front of the door to barricade us in. There was nobody after us! Yet I was running from someone, from something. I ask myself often, what was I hiding from? The answer is I was running from myself.

There was a fight on the inside and my spirit and flesh was warring against each other. Which is why when we become saved we have to make sure that our spirit is "saved" and transformed. What good is it we're just having a brief emotional experience that change our feelings for the moment, but our heart is not changed? Our relationship with the Holy Spirit makes all of the difference. Our salvation is contained in the work of the Holy Spirit dear one. Listen to the Apostle Paul on this subject:

Galatians 5:16-18

16*This I say then, Walk in the Spirit, and ye shall not fulfil the lust of the flesh.* 17*For the flesh lusteth against the Spirit, and the Spirit against the flesh: and these are contrary the* *one to the other: so that ye cannot do the things that ye would.* **18***But if ye be led of the Spirit, ye are not under the law.*

Don't focus on the lack in your life. Focus on how in Christ, you are complete in everything right now at this very moment. Let the Spirit lead you in all things so that you can experience the fullness of God's love in this life.

Sometimes we step out of line and we have to pay the consequence for these actions. I was so lost during that time in my life that I stooped so low as to visit a psychic. Can you believe that? As a child of God, I went to a psychic. I was still trapped in the darkness dear one, yet I was in the light. And God instructed me to pen this body of work because I know that some of you are trapped in a dark room, a wretched and hellish place as well.

But I'm here to tell you that you don't have to stay there, because God is a deliverer! I'm not fooled or impressed by titles. I'm not fooled or impressed by what church you attend. I'm not fooled or impressed by how many scriptures you can recite or how well you speak in tongues, because I know that you can do all of these things and still be trapped. You can remain trapped in your emotions. You can remain trapped in your mentality. You can remain trapped in your sexuality. You can be trapped to the point of almost suffering psychosis. You can just remain trapped. But the revelation behind our seemingly unchangeable situations is that the door is always open even when we're sitting in the prison of our circumstances. When we don't move past our experiences and circumstances our minds become veiled and only the power of God can remove this veil.

I did all of those wretched things because my mind was veiled and my spirit was crying out for someone to remove it. When I got saved at sixteen it wasn't because I had reached my zenith in God, it was because I was searching for an something to complete me. I was looking for love from anybody who would give it to me. I was desperate and when I heard about Jesus, the lover of my soul, I opened myself up to Him as well.

Which is why I truly believe that you have to open yourself up to God and allow His Spirit to permeate your very being. The scriptures say in 2 Corinthians 3 that *where the Spirit of the Lord is there is liberty.*

2 Corinthians 16-18

16*But whenever anyone turns to the Lord, the veil is taken*
away. **17***Now the Lord is the Spirit, and where the Spirit of*
the Lord is, there is freedom. **18***And we all, who with unveiled*
faces contemplate the Lord's glory, are being transformed

into his image with ever-increasing glory, which comes from the Lord, who is the Spirit.

I can say today that because my God is Spirit, He was able to do surgery on the inside of me and deliver me from my fears. He was able to deliver me from my depression. He was able to deliver me from my pain. And most importantly He was able to deliver me from myself. A deliverer is one who sets free or saves another from a difficult situation. And I can praise God today because one of the most vivid pictures of God in the Bible is that of being our Deliverer. Take it from me dear one, He is!

Just as our Lord Jesus descended into hell to take back the keys of life and death from satan, He can descend to whatever depth that you find yourself in man of God or woman of God and He's strong enough to pull you out. Just like He hopped in the pit with Joseph and promoted Him to the palace, He can and will do the same for you, as long as you allow your spirit to be changed and directed by the Holy Spirit. You might be in a valley right now, but look to the hills from where your help comes. You help comes from the Lord, the maker of Heaven and Earth and He will not allow your feet to be moved.

Please allow me to leave you with this passage of scripture from **Psalms 91:14-16** because I believe that there is an anointing on this book, and I declare that the reader of this book is about to be rescued by the lover of your soul**:**

14 *"Because he loves me," says the Lord, "I will rescue him;*
I will protect him, for he acknowledges my name.
15 *He will call on me, and I will answer him; I will be with*
him in trouble, I will deliver him and honor him.
16 *With long life I will satisfy him and show him my*
salvation."

CHAPTER 4

AN ANTS PREPARATION

Proverbs 6:6-8

*[6] Go to the ant, thou sluggard; consider her ways, and be
wise: [7] Which having no guide, overseer, or ruler,
[8]Provideth her meat in the summer, and gathereth her food
in the harvest.*

The number one best way to ensure that lack never occurs is preparation. Solomon tells us in the book of Proverbs to consider the ants in that they gather their food in the summer time, so that during the winter time they will have enough food.

The ants are one of the most impressive creatures on earth. We could even study them as a people if we wanted to. Whereas they have houses, towns, public roads and show their wisdom and prudence by preparing their meat in due season. The ability to understand and prepare for the seasons that will be low is what I most admire about the ants.

Likewise, in a spiritual capacity, we as men and women of God need to do the same thing. If we are honest there are times in our lives when what we see in the natural doesn't correlate to what we've heard from God in the spiritual. And at these times is when we should be able to rely on our faith.

However if our faith has not been build up then we won't have anything to rely on. The Bible says Faith cometh by hearing, and hearing by the Word of God. So if we don't have a lot of the Word in us then we will find ourselves being shaken. When our money gets funny and the rent or mortgage is due, we have to be able to rely on our already built up, and stored up faith. Somebody is going through a season right now and you need to shout "Faith don't fail me now!"

The Word of God is the will of God and the only way to get

it right is to read it. Leaders are readers and when we read God's Word it authorizes our spirit to be blessed with more of Him. More of His direction. More of His love. More of His wisdom. More of His understanding. Reading the Word of God fills you with more of Him.

God slowly pulled me out of the pit that I found myself in by downloading His kingdom purpose in me. There are showers of blessings and favor when we walk in obedience, according to God's purpose for our lives. When I gave up my need to control. And to take it a little bit further, when I gave up my anger regarding the past things that I couldn't control, I was finally able to enjoy a season of rest from self-effort.

Dear one, in Christ, it is a finished work. In His presence there is fullness of joy. New mercy in abundance and great grace and peace in this obedience season is what He wants to transfer to you.

Peace is attainable. Don't allow anyone to tell you anything different. You must first create your environment of peace, then place yourself in what I like to call a peace bubble. If you keep yourself in the peace bubble anything that tries to hit you will first have to penetrate and burst the peace bubble. You deserve to get your peace back. Protect your peace at all costs and live in peace on purpose.

Best thing I have ever done for myself is to let go of trying to control my life and commit to doing it God's way. Sometimes I can hardly fathom how He made glory out of such a mess, and I'm referring to myself, but I'm so glad that He did.

The thing that I do know, is that He prepared me for it. Every experience that we live through in life prepares us for our next experience. That's why instead of complaining about the things that you don't understand you should ask God for the wisdom that you were meant to gain from it.

Just as you're not supposed to paint a wall before you put the primer on, is the same way that God uses one experience to prepare for the next. So stop complaining about the primer because God is getting ready to apply the paint men and women of God. If He doesn't prepare you than the paint won't be applied correctly, it will be blotchy, and the end result won't be proper. The paint will be wasted. The wall will be ugly. And the effort will be useless. So appreciate the primer.

When you complain it means that you don't appreciate the primer. There are two main reasons why we complain. We complain because we feel powerless and we complain because it becomes habitual.

The reason why you feel powerless is because you've taken the burden upon yourself. The burdens that can really hurt us and sometimes kill us are way too much for us to bear. That's why God said this in the book of Psalms:

Psalms 55:22

Cast thy burden upon the LORD, and he shall sustain thee: he shall never suffer the righteous to be moved.

We have replaced the Church of God with going to Church. We have replaced being the Church, with having Church. The truth is that we are the church and God's will can only manifest to the world as we be God's mouthpiece as well as His hands, feet, eyes, ears.

I will repeat that the feeling of powerlessness sometimes lead to a complaining spirit. For example, the economy has shaken a lot of people's foundations and many of them feel powerless regarding this fact and if you listen very carefully, you will recognize that many of them, and sometimes us if we're honest, have become habitual complainers. Wake up church because this is not the conduct of the Kingdom.

. I believe that God is beginning to awaken the true church The era of the traditional, religious, manmade Church is coming to an end. The church is not the four walls that so many obsess about and in some cases idolize, the true church is us and the true church is only now manifesting. Are you a member of the true church? The true church are the children of God who have come to the realization of the their true and authentic selves, their true and authentic identity, and have died enough to self that God has entrusted and commissioned them to release His authority and power on the earth.

We must understand that it is God that is forming His church and it's only by God's power that we, His church, will be successful.

Zechariah 4:6

"Then he answered and spake unto me saying, This is the word of the Lord unto Zerubbabel, saying, Not by might, nor by power, but by my spirit, saith the Lord of hosts"

Just as military might and human power could not accomplish the rebuilding of the temple during Zechariah's time, neither will human intellect or any other high thing be able to exalt itself against the knowledge of God in this season.. God had to use workers empowered by His Spirit under the direction and leadership of Zerubbabel to rebuild the temple and we need to be empowered by the Spirit of God, and follow the directives and leadership of the Spirit of God to be able to operate in the authority that God has given us in the earth.

As God is waking us up I believe that explosions of the manifestation of God's Glory are about to take place and that we will walk in our God given authority and power in the earth! This is my prayer in Jesus' name, Amen!

Now watch this, just like the ants we need to prepare for the manifestation. Seasons in the natural world change gradually, however seasons in the spirit world changes suddenly. And we must be ready.

Build yourselves up in your faith because during the lean times we still have to be able to provide an explanation of the hope that lies within us to whoever requires it. Even in the times when it feels like winter and we can't see things growing that normally grow and blossom we must be complete, not lacking nothing.

As I stated in the first chapter, the biggest place that we are attacked is our mind. So that is why our faith meter has to be high and maintained. One way of doing this is by not allowing people to rent space in our head.
In the natural we would not allow a person to rent an apartment or a house from us that couldn't demonstrate an ability to pay the fees. Likewise, don't allow anyone to rent space in your head, unless they're a good tenant.

What I mean by that is that if they're not moving you towards your purpose, don't have meaningful communications with them. If there is a person in your life that every time after you speak to them or meet with them you start to doubt yourself or begin to have negative thoughts concerning what you were once sure about, you need to do yourself a favor and limit your conversation with them. I don't care if you have to put ear plugs in your ears every time they come around you. Do what you have to do to inoculate yourself against their venom in your mind and it will be easier for you to remain in faith.

It will be easier for you to remain a vessel, full of faith, and full of confidence.

Spiritual maturity is not measured by how high you jump in praise but by how straight you walk in obedience. If we simply obey God's instructions, which are contained in His Word, we can never go wrong. Consider a scripture out of Paul's letter to Philippi in the book of Philippians that tells us how to think:

Philippians 4:8

Finally, brethren, whatsoever things are true, whatsoever things are honest, whatsoever things are just, whatsoever things are pure, whatsoever things are lovely, whatsoever things are of good report; if there be any virtue, and if there be any praise, think on these things.

It is clear that God didn't want to leave anything to chance which is why He inspired Paul to pen this letter for our benefit. If it isn't positive then it's not welcome. Protect what God has placed on the inside of you on purpose and without apology.

So, I want to end this chapter by encouraging you to go on a complaining fast. Not because it will make everyone around you happier, although it will, but because it will help you experience more happiness, joy, peace, success and positive relationships.

As soon as you start feeling the urge to complain, identify if you are fighting with a feeling of powerlessness and hopelessness and rebuke those spirits far from you, because that's what they really are. For we wrestle not against flesh and blood, but principalities and powers and rulers of darkness in high places.

CHAPTER 5

NOTHING MISSING, NOTHING LACKING

Job 5:24

You will know that your tent is secure; you will take stock of your property and find nothing missing.

The above words were spoken by Eliphaz the Temanite, when he finally responded to Job's tirade of cursing the day he was born in the second chapter of the book of Job, because of the God allowed troubles in his life.

After Job was stricken with boils and sores the Bible says

that he sat down and scraped them all off. His wife told him to curse God and die, because she felt that he didn't do anything to deserve what he was going through. However, he told her to be quiet and called her foolish. The same response that Job had to the foolishness of his wife at that time is the same response that we need to have to anyone that tells us to give up and blame God for what we're going through.

The truth of the matter is that Job really was blameless in the sight of God but satan, the accuser of the brethren, went to God and alleged that the only reason that he was faithful to God is because nothing ever went wrong.

We need to apply the truth of our this story to our own lives in that maybe some of the trials that we're going through right now could be because of our good in the eyes of God, not because of our bad or inadequacies.

What do you do when you know that you're doing everything right, but things still go wrong? You trust God just like Job did and never allow yourself to forget that God sees all and will judge righteously. See in everything that was going on in Job's life the Bible goes on record that he still didn't sin. Look at the text:

Job 2:9-10

9His wife said to him, "Are you still maintaining your integrity? Curse God and die!"
10He replied, "You are talking like a foolishb woman. Shall we accept good from God, and not trouble?"
In all this, Job did not sin in what he said.

How can we expect to go through life without ever experiencing things that we wouldn't choose for ourselves. Shall we accept good from God and not trouble? The Bible is clear in letting us understand that some of the tough things that we go through are from God, not from the enemy. So our response should still be one of integrity and without sin before God. You're issues is not an excuse to sin dear one. Your calamity is not a license to forget who you are. Every morning we need to put on the helmet of salvation and remind ourselves daily as we encounter things that would make us forget.

The mind is a secret enclosure of which nothing can enter it unless you allow it and you must never allow doubt and blame to contaminate your walk with the Lord. Your mind, your mental state can leave you in lack even when you should be lacking nothing. Remember the promises of God in that He wishes above all that you should prosper and be in good health even as your soul prospers. Remember that He answers the prayers of the righteous and is far from the wicked and that He is fair regarding the things that He allows in this world and in Heaven.

Keep praying to yourself, "Thy Kingdom come, Thy will be done." And don't allow the words to be just mere words. Let it be truly the way you think. Giving up your way of thinking about things and trusting that God must have a reason and a plan shows humility and a surrendering to God. Remember, as a man thinks, so is he. Watch your thoughts because a healthy mindset normally equates to a healthy body and spirt.

Now, let me take you to another person that seemed like he had it all, but was still missing something. His name was Naaman:

2 Kings 5 (NKJV)

5 *Now Naaman, commander of the army of the king of Syria, was a great and honorable man in the eyes of his master, because by him the Lord had given victory to Syria. He was also a mighty man of valor, but a leper.*

And what do you do when it seems like you have it all but something is still missing? You put your best foot forward anyway realizing that it's only by God's grace that you have what you do have, anyway.

Naaman was a big time commander. He was basically a four star general if we were to equate him to our modern day rank structure in the United States Army; however he was a leper. And lepers were scorned and ostracized during that period of history. So the fact that he was so successful in his career went totally against the issues that he was having in his personal life. But the Bible says that he was known as a man of honor.

No matter what you're dealing with never forget that you are carrying around the glory of God within you and how you represent Him should only bring Him glory, honor, and praise.

[2] *And the Syrians had gone out on raids, and had brought*
back captive a young girl from the land of Israel. She waited
on Naaman's wife. [3] *Then she said to her mistress, "If only*
my master were with the prophet who is in Samaria! For he
would heal him of his leprosy." [4] *And Naaman went in and*
told his master, saying, "Thus and thus said the girl

who is from the land of Israel."

God always has a resource, a connection, a way out as long as you just keep enduring. Leprosy was a death sentence and Naaman could've used it as an excuse to be nothing. But he kept on being the best that he could be.

The result of the good rapport that Naaman had garnered with the King of Syria is that the king sent a letter on Naaman's behalf to the King of Syria. The lesson is those that you serve well will almost always bless you back if they're given the opportunity. Which is why you should always treat others the way that you want to be treated; even in a service capacity. When you treat others with respect and integrity they have no choice but to speak well of you.

The King of Syria showed great character because the true test of character is how you treat someone that can absolutely do nothing back for you in return. This is the true measure of a man or woman.

You also have to know where your help comes from. And Naaman clearly understood that the King of Syria was in his corner. Start implementing the wisdom of Naaman dear one.

Roll with those who support you not tolerate you. Your victory will probably depend on it. Your healing might be connected to it. Your breakthrough will be based on the people that God has put in your life to help you reach the next level of greatness in Him.

Greatness has no problem with submitting to greatness and we see that even though Naaman was highly respected and a general and all of these things he still humbled himself and showed respect to someone that was greater than him. He still asked the opinion and for the help of the master that God had placed over him. And because of this humbleness of spirit, God, through the King of Syria rewarded him. When we remain humble, God in His timing, will honor us. God will make sure that we are lacking no good thing.

So let me encourage you to get over yourself today and figure out who, what, or where it is that God wants to use to bless you and to help you. Submit to the process because when you really look at it God's way your purpose will start becoming more clear.

Just as we see in Naaman's story, healing comes with recommendation, so protect your genuine relationships and never burn bridges because you never know who you will need in the future to make it.

Now, I want to conclude this chapter just be taking you to what must have been going on in the inside of Naaman when he heard that there was a chance for him to be healed and made whole. Maybe you have been living a life of incompleteness. Never feeling like you've had it all together. Maybe you've been dealing with issues since your youth because of things done to you or not done to you and you thing that there is no help or ability for you to be restored.

I'm here to tell you that restoration lies in Jesus Christ. And in Him there is nothing lacking. If you have a hole in your heart because of broken trusts, Jesus wants to mend it. If you have self-esteem issues because you've always been treated as second class, you need to know that Jesus thinks so highly of you that He left His heavenly habitation to come to earth simply so He could forfeit His life for yours. Let me introduce you to Jesus, the author, and finisher of our faith, with the words of Paul as he wrote to the church of Colosse in Colossians chapter 1 verses 9-23..

Preeminence of Christ

9 For this reason we also, since the day we heard it, do not cease to pray for you, and to ask that you may be filled with the knowledge of His will in all wisdom and spiritual understanding; 10 that you may walk worthy of the Lord, fully pleasing Him, being fruitful in every good work and increasing in the knowledge of God; 11 strengthened with all might, according to His glorious power, for all patience and longsuffering with joy; 12 giving thanks to the Father who has qualified us to be partakers of the inheritance of the saints in the light. 13 He has delivered us from the power of darkness and conveyed us into the kingdom of the Son of His love, 14 in whom we have redemption through His blood,[c] the forgiveness of sins.

15 He is the image of the invisible God, the firstborn over all creation. 16 For by Him all things were created that are in heaven and that are on earth, visible and invisible, whether thrones or dominions or principalities or powers. All things were created through Him and for Him. 17 And He is before all things, and in Him all things consist. 18 And He is the head of the body, the church, who is the beginning, the firstborn from the dead, that in all things He may have the preeminence.

Reconciled in Christ

19 For it pleased the Father that in Him all the fullness should dwell, 20 and by Him to reconcile all things to Himself, by Him, whether things on earth or things in heaven, having made peace through the blood of His cross.

21 And you, who once were alienated and enemies in your mind by wicked works, yet now He has reconciled 22 in the body of His flesh through death, to present you holy, and blameless, and above reproach in His sight— 23 if indeed you continue in the faith, grounded and steadfast, and are not moved away from the hope of the gospel which you heard, which was preached to every creature under heaven, of which I, Paul, became a minister.

CHAPTER 6

STAY CONNECTED

Jeremiah 23:4

[4]And I will set up shepherds over them which shall feed them: and they shall fear no more, nor be dismayed, neither shall they be lacking, saith the LORD.

Every sheep needs a shepherd. One of the biggest ways to be truly complete in God is by staying in His presence. Being a part of a well fed flock of men and women of God who love the Word of God and are being taught the raw unadulterated Word of God is so vital.

I want to help someone in this chapter because many of us have gone through one of those seasons where we think that we don't need church, a pastor, or anyone other than ourselves to be in God and grow. But I'm here to tell you that this is one of the most subtle tricks of the enemy. He wants to keep you disconnected from any God ordained fellowship or ministry. Recognize his attempts and don't allow it.

The Bible tells us in Hebrews 10:25 to forsake not the assembly of ourselves together.

Hebrews 10:25 (KJV)

[25] *Not forsaking the assembling of ourselves together, as the manner of some is; but exhorting one another: and so much the more, as ye see the day approaching.*

The trick of the enemy is to keep you unplugged from the source. An iron is a very useful accommodation to have in any household to get the wrinkles out of skirts, shirts or any other clothing, however, if the iron is not plugged up, no heat will be generated and the iron will be inoperable. The same thing applies to us when we are not under the hearing of God's Word. We slowly start cooling off to where we become ineffective.

Signs of you cooling off could be that you start talking about your church or the church in general. You can always tell when someone has had a change of heart recently concerning certain things when you hear someone talking about their pastor and their congregation. Why? Because it's one thing to walk away from something but it's another thing to talk bad about it. The Bible says touch not my anointed and do my prophets no harm, and we need to know that when we are speaking negatively about the man or woman of God we are, in fact, touching God's anointed, and God is not impressed.

When we're speaking against God's called and chosen we are in fact propagating malice against the Kingdom of God because we are planting seeds in the hearts of the hearers that sometimes will never be uprooted, and God is not impressed. These actions initiates a curse against us and we can't expect to have the full blessings of God while we're in this antagonistic state against God.

Don't let malice keep you out of the palace. The Law Dictionary demonstrates that the word malice itself is not just ill will but an intentional and wrongful act against someone without a justified excuse, thereby defining "malicious intent." It is a violation of the law by someone that works to the prejudice of another person. If you are in lack or if it just seems like you can never get it all together. Maybe you should ask yourself a question. Who are you in malice against?

See, God doesn't kick us out of His plans, it is our disobedience that causes us to be thrust out of His plan. When you disconnect from the source, which is God's Word, you become disconnected from its power.

The Word is alive. **Hebrews 4:12** says that the *Word is quicker and powerful than any two-edged sword, dividing to the asunder of soul and spirit.* And when you start putting the power of the living Word to action it produces power in your spirit that causes you to instantly be made whole.

A person that is full of the Word is not depressed, mad, or bitter. A person that has a steady diet of the Word of God is complete in their spirit, and not lacking any good thing. A person that is under the constant hearing of the Word of God is steady and stable. The person who shuns the things of God are the most unstable people on earth. Get full of the Word dear one. Eat it, digest it, and regurgitate it and then eat it again. Get fat in your spirit with a healthy diet of God's Word.

The individuals that are walking around malnourished normally have developed a spirit of malice against the church, the Word of God, and God's people and they're always looking for other anorexic Christians. Don't be a member of this group dear one. This is the one time where it's okay to eat too much dear one and I guarantee you that you will never be in better shape and that you will never be more beautiful.

I like something that I heard the late and great, Bishop Eddie Long, preach one day. He said " The devil ain't trying to kill you. He's just trying to take your faith." And just like that statement we must not be put off of by the diversions that the enemy of our souls tries to throw at us. It's not going to kill you it's just going to make your faith in God stronger. Like the old saying says, "Whatever don't kill you, makes you stronger."
We must marshal our feelings to line up with our purpose. The enemy's job is to try and kill you but he's on a leash and is still working for God even though he doesn't look at it that way. If God wanted you dead, you would already be so. So

cheer up somebody. You're still here so that means that God still has more for you to do. God still has purpose for your life!

That sickness wasn't sent to kill you, because God's Word over your life is more powerful than the enemies threats. The infirmity was sent to kill your faith not you, so get up! Just because you're going through a season of scarcity right now doesn't mean that God is not going to supply all of your needs because the attack wasn't sent to take you out, it was sent to take your faith.

If God be for us who can be against us? Don't allow the severity of the attack to intimidate you. Also don't allow your faith to go up and down with how good or bad you feel, just maintain your faith. Don't be distracted by how serious it seems right now just remember that God is the source of your strength and He is the strength of your life and He will come through for you. Consider the words of Habakkuk.

Habakkuk 3:19

19 The LORD God is my strength, and he will make my feet like hinds' feet, and he will make me to walk upon mine high places.

Yes, sometimes we get bruised and sometimes we get a little battered even as children of God but don't run from the darkness. Don't run from the problems. Run to the light and let Him shine on your situation. Keep the faith in God's Word and the fact that He cannot be beaten. This is crux of what I'm saying in this section of message to you dear one. Our faith is not a figment of someone's imagination it is factual. The Word of God is true. Everything that God has taught us is true and our most built up faith is in fact, factual. My faith is factual. Christianity is not a religion it is a relationship. And what we believe is true. If you're not sure about this or if you at any time start to waiver in your faith, it means you are disconnected.

John 15:5

I am the vine; you are the branches. If you remain in me and I in you, you will bear much fruit; apart from me you can do nothing.

There are 86,400 seconds in every day. How many of these seconds are we actively connected to the source, which is the vine, as described by Jesus Himself in John 15:5. So many of us don't mind vegging out to secular music, or mindless TV programming or junk magazines and more. But how many of us really make a conscious decision to stay connected to the source?

What if we stay plugged in and connected to our Creator with the same unmatched enthusiasm? What if we were to give God the same dedication, reliance and trust that we give to all of these other venues and distractions. Jesus is the vine and we are the branches. If we remain in Jesus, we're connected to the source and according to the Word of God we'll be able to do anything in God's will.

One of the ways that God has given us to get connected is prayer. When we wake up we should pray, whereas we are booting up to the source from our most earliest thoughts. God is the power source that we have to access to receive power. And by us being the branches stemming from the vine we are plugging into God when we pray and simultaneously we become fully functional as a result.

Pray early in the morning and late at night men and women of God. And I'd also like to strongly suggest that prayer should be implemented throughout the day as well. The Bible says pray without ceasing. Whatever you do, never stop praying, because prayer keeps you connected.

Prayer inevitably leads to worship and when a person truly enters into worship it's gets so good that it can be hard to exit from such a cerebral time in God. A true worshipper doesn't stop and sometimes can't stop until they touch the heart of God. And when you pick your private and intimate times of prayer well enough you won't have to stop until your spirit is full and you are sure that God is really pleased.

When you stay connected to the Holy Spirit and closely united with your heavenly Father all the power of heaven is at your disposal. You will be able to ask what you will and Heaven will make a way for you. Are you seeing the value of being connected yet?

The last piece of advice that I'll give you on the subject of staying connected in this particular section of this body of work is that to stay connected you have to guard against every form of compromise in your life.

Refuse to allow worldly things and ambitions to steal away your time with God. Don't allow earthly anxieties, worry, power, career, ungodly ambitions, love interests, or any kind of relationship to compete with your relationship with God.

Do you know that relationships with saved individuals

can be a distraction just as much or more so than a relationship with an unsaved individual? Not everything with a label on it that appears to say God, is good. Remember that. Not everything that seems to be Godly is of God.

One of the biggest tricks of the enemy is counterfeit and imitation. From the garden satan has been trying to counterfeit the power of God and more importantly, His purpose and will. He challenged Eve in her faith with the blending of truth with a lie.

First, he asked Eve about the directives she had been given, to see if she knew the truth. When she replied correctly, he went a little deeper to input seeds of doubt. If the enemy can make you start questioning the will of God concerning you, you have just given him some of the highest worship that he craves. He craves to create like God and he craves to instill purpose like God. Since he can't do both, he has to imitate and defraud. He'll take it any way he can get it saints.

Remember Jeremiah 29:11 men and women of God and guard against the compromise.

Jeremiah 29:11 (KJV)

[11] For I know the thoughts that I think toward you, saith the Lord, thoughts of peace, and not of evil, to give you an expected end.

CHAPTER 7

USE WHAT IS IN YOUR HAND

Exodus 4:1-3

1Then Moses said, "What if they will not believe me or listen to what I say? For they may say, 'The LORD has not appeared to you.'" 2The LORD said to him, "What is that in your hand?" And he said, "A staff." 3Then He said, "Throw it on the ground." So he threw it on the ground, and it became a serpent; and Moses fled from it.

Imagine being called up by the President of the United States and being asked to come serve on his cabinet. The future of the entire country is on the line, and he wants your assistance. What would you do? What would you say?

This is what was happening to Moses. Moses found Himself in a conversation with the one who knows all things and God was saying that He had need of him. And just like Moses' encounter with God, we need to understand that God has need of us and guess what's good about this fact? If God has called you to it, it's His job to get you through it. So He has to provide you with the means to win.

If you don't get but one thing out of this book, I want it to be that prevision always precedes provision. God has equipped you with everything you need already. God always equips us those who are His with what we need to be who we're meant to be, just like Moses.

God equips us to be champions over our circumstances. And we just have to discover what it is that we have in our hand and then start applying it. Let me encourage you to use your talents and abilities to serve Him.

For me personally, life was throwing me hard balls left and right, but because I didn't know that I had a bat, I kept getting hit. God gave me the revelation that I'm supposed to be equipped with everything that I need to win the battle, just like Moses. And that's when I noticed the staff in my hand.

God showed me the bat in my hand and then I started swinging.

Our bat is the Word of God. No matter what is lobbed our way, we can smack it back with the Word of God. God has equipped you to handle difficult things, all you have to do is use your bat. There is no fast ball that the Bible can't smack back.

What you have is more than enough. Your talent is already enough. The way you speak is already more than enough. Your mental capacity is more than enough. Your innate abilities and whatever God has blessed you with is what you're supposed to use make it in this life and more importantly be a blessing. So, stop making things difficult.

Moses though that he didn't have anything to complete his God given assignment. And that's why you should never compare your weaknesses to another person's strengths. Little in the hands of God is much.

Now watch this, what Moses had was nothing until he used it for God. The other thing was that had to use what God designed for him to be successful. Moses used to use a sword when he was a general in Pharaoh's army. But God allowed some things to move him from one team to the next.

As long as Moses used God's instrument he was victorious. Was Moses' rod a lucky charm? No. But God was able to use what Moses had to reveal His power.

Now, we all have something that can be used by God, however, what we have is nothing until we give it to God. Consider the little boy with five small barley loaves and two small fish in John chapter 6. What the boy had was nothing until he gave it to God. The boy gave all he had, and Jesus multiplied it and used it for His glory.

Was five loaves and two fish enough to feed a multitude? No. But he gave what he had to God and God was able to use it despite its size. God will use whatever you give Him dear one in spite of the level and aptitude of the actual gift.

God will use the unseemingly to make the enemy look bad. Let's look at Sansom.

Judges 15:14-17

[14]*As he approached Lehi, the Philistines came toward him shouting. The Spirit of the Lord came powerfully upon him.*

The ropes on his arms became like charred flax, and the bindings dropped from his hands. [15]Finding a fresh jawbone of a donkey, he grabbed it and struck down a thousand men. [16]Then Samson said, "With a donkey's jawbone I have made donkeys of them. With a donkey's jawbone I have killed a thousand men." [17]When he finished speaking, he threw away the jawbone; and the place was called Ramath Lehi.

What Samson had was nothing until he used it for God. Is a donkey's jawbone a powerful killing tool? No. But God was able to use it to His glory. When you are operating in your purpose, God will bless whatever you use, because you were created to win. You're a winner and God will pull some strings to make sure you do.

What do you have to offer to God? Is it much? The crux of the lessons behind these stories is not about a magic rod, a multiplied lunch, or a tough jawbone. The focus is on the majesty of a mighty, all powerful, God who can use whatever you have, if you give it to Him. Have you made that commitment? Does God have all of you, and all you have? Imagine what God could do with what you have. Give it over to Him today.

Give your prayer life over to Him and watch God start

answering all of your prayers. Give your family over to Him and watch your family start thriving and coming together. Give your business over to Him and watch your business start growing. Give your ministry over to Him and watch God start enlarging your territory and opening up new opportunities that only He can open. Give it over to Him. Let me leave you with this benediction

Hebrews 13:20-21

[20]Now may the God of peace, who through the blood of the eternal covenant brought back from the dead our Lord Jesus, the great Shepherd of the sheep, [21]equip you with every good thing to do His will. And may He accomplish in us what is pleasing in His sight through Jesus Christ, to whom be glory forever and ever. Amen.

CHAPTER 8

OUR SECURE PLACE IN GOD

1 John 2:1-2

[1]*My little children, I am writing these things to you so that you will not sin. But if anyone does sin, we have an advocate before the Father — Jesus Christ, the Righteous One.* [2]*He Himself is the atoning sacrifice for our sins, and not for ours alone, but also for the sins of the whole world.*

When we as Christians make mistakes, we do not lose our place as a son or daughter of God, but what does happen is that we jeopardize our fellowship with Him. I had to learn that whenever I found myself in sin presumptuously or mistakenly, I was shunning the presence of God because He can't reside in sin.

I'm glad of the knowledge that I've acquired regarding this fact because this is one of the biggest ways that the enemy uses to keep us bound. We all undoubtedly sin at some point of our walk with God, however, we should also know that we have an attorney in Heaven that is always fighting for us to put us back in right standing.

Jesus is our Family Lawyer. Whenever we make a mistake and our fellowship is broken, He stands at the right hand of the Father and starts interceding for us. We can immediately go to God about our behaviors. He will help us to get back on our feet, forgive us, and help us not to make the same mistake again.

In Old Testament times, defending the accused was such a sacred duty that the judge refused to delegate the work to an attorney. The Judge himself, would serve as the defender of the accused. The study of Jewish history lets us know that Attorneys at law were non-existent. Their legal code required the judges to "lean always to the side of the defendant and give him the advantage of every possible doubt."

Isn't it good to know that Jesus, Himself, is our advocate? The beauty behind Him being our lawyer, is the fact that we have to know and understand that He cannot lose. It doesn't matter how dirty we've gotten and how far from God we have removed ourselves, Jesus will argue our case.

When I learned of the Jewish custom of the actual judge deliberating the case it just made me that much more relaxed in the fact that I won't have to rely on anyone else ability other than Jesus Himself, and that is simply awesome. My soul is at rest.

At times, there is a place that God prepares for just you and Him and it is your responsibility to be there when God is there. If you're not careful you will blame others for not "being there" but we should blame no one but ourselves when we are not at the appointed place when God expects us to be there.

One of the basics of any kind of success is self-discipline and for us to be on time for anything let alone an encounter with God is on us. When we are constantly late it shows a lack of regard for whoever we're supposed to meet. Or it shows disrespect for whatever place or organization that we're supposed to be at. This reflects poorly on us and is a hint to having less than honorable character and God does not make provision for our slothfulness.

I'm writing this because God doesn't want us to be in lack at all and this is one of the ways that we sometimes get ourselves in trouble. Our position determines our condition and when we're late and out of position how can God bless our position?

On the other hand sometimes it is the hand of God keeping us from some things. Maybe it was the hand of God that closed the door. Sometimes He closes the door behind you so that you and Him can have an intimate moment. Maybe He closed the door so that you can learn to trust Him and know He is your source.

Maybe He has closed a few doors to prepare you for an assignment that is much greater than where you are right now. So instead of focusing on where you are, focus on where you are going. And when you arrive, instead of focusing on who is not there, focus on the one who is there. The great I Am, El Shaddai, Jehovah Shammah, which means the Lord is there!

God Himself defends and judges the accused. But who is the accuser? Revelation 12:10 speaks of the devil who accuses us before God day and night. Our enemy also keeps a record of sin, and his accusations are painfully correct most of the times. So the question is how do we then overcome these accusations?

We overcome him by the blood of the Lamb and by the word of our testimony.

Revelation 12:11 NIV
They overcame him by the blood of the Lamb and by the word of their testimony.

Jesus' priestly work as our Advocate, is what guarantees that we will arrive at the place of our purpose without delay. 1 John 2:1 explains, involves our ongoing sanctification and our once-for-all justification. When we first trust Jesus, His righteousness is imputed to us, giving us a righteous status that cannot be lost as it shows in Romans 5:9 and in Romans 8:30.

Romans 5:9 (ESV)

[9] Since, therefore, we have now been justified by his blood, much more shall we be saved by him from the wrath of God.

Romans 8:30 (ESV)

[30] And those whom he predestined he also called, and those whom he called he also justified, and those whom he justified he also glorified.

Yet even though there is no condemnation for those who are in Christ Jesus, we're human, so we continue to sin until we are glorified. We continually need God's forgiveness to encourage us to walk in holiness. As we repent, Jesus advocates for us to restore our fellowship with God.

Even now, Jesus is pleading with the Father in our behalf, interceding for us that we might be forgiven, purified, and strengthened for holiness. Now don't make any mistakes because we work out our salvation in fear and trembling as it says in Philippians 2:12–13,

Philippians 2:12–13 (ESV)

[12] Therefore, my beloved, as you have always obeyed, so now, not only as in my presence but much more in my

absence, work out your own salvation with fear and trembling, **13** *for it is God who works in you, both to will and to work for his good pleasure.*

But even as we're working out our salvation with fear and trembling we can be confident and even bold. We can do so because the Savior prays for us to guarantee our perseverance. Let us rejoice that Jesus continues to advocate for us, and let us always draw near to the throne of grace when we are in need.

Why am I writing so extensively on this? Because the sooner that we can grab hold to the liberty that we have in Christ, the sooner that we can live as such. We're bound because we living under the curse of the law, but in Christ, the advocate for our every transgression, we are free. We're no longer under the law dear one, we're under grace. Somebody needs to give God praise for this fact right now. Hallelujah!

CHAPTER 9

FINISHERS GRACE

Romans 8:13

For if you live according to the flesh, you will die; but if by the Spirit you put to death the deeds of the body, you will live.

In order for any of the information that I'm sharing with you to work dear one you will have to pray for what I will term as a finisher's grace.

There was a man who undergoing hypnosis to lose weight. One of his friends asked him if he thought it would work. The guy's response was, "Well it worked last time."

Which basically is indicating that if he has to do it again, then no, it didn't work.

We can all start things well but it doesn't mean know how to finish what we started. Case in point is that many people get married and are so excited at their wedding only to have these emotions dissipate over time and walk away from their marriage. We have to pray to God for the grace and strength to endure in the process of life not just to make aimless resolutions. Not just to make yet another declaration that we have no intent of maintaining.

Learn to have resolve so that you won't have to make resolutions. People who continually make new resolutions are people that are admitting that they need a new start. However, individuals who have resolve, don't have to repeatedly make new starts because their resolve is a byproduct of their self-discipline which translates into a way of life, not an every new year fix.

Let's face it starting well is relatively easy, finishing well is a different matter. Just like starting a new diet or exercise. In the beginning these things can be fun, but after a while these "fun" things can be the bane of our existence if we're honest.

The same is true of being a Christian. Becoming a Christian is relatively easy. All we have to do is acknowledge to God that we are sinners and receive by faith the free gift of eternal life that Christ provided by His shed blood. Salvation is not free because Jesus paid for our salvation with his innocently shed blood, but He did all of the work, so for us we can't earn it or work for it.

But then after all of that comes the hard part. Because then we have to stick in there as Christians in a world that is openly hostile towards God and His people. What do you do when the world is showing you all of its benefits and dangling all of the pleasures of the flesh in front of you? Even though we know that these things are in opposition of God we have to admit that sometimes there is a certain temptation. However, as long as we are secure and complete on the inside the temptation on the outside will not prevail.

From within, the flesh entices you to forsake Christ and gratify your sinful desires. The enemy hits you with temptation after temptation. The real test of your faith is, will you endure? If you have genuine faith in Christ, you will persevere to the end. There is no finish line, unless we look at the finish line as taking our very last breath in this earth realm. Consider Paul at the end of his earthly ministry and life:

2 Timothy 4:7-8

7*I have fought the good fight, I have finished the race, I have kept the faith.* **8***From now on the crown of righteousness is laid up for me, which the Lord, the righteous judge, will award to me on that day—and not only to me, but to all who crave His appearing.*

Paul, undoubtedly, had a finisher's grace. At one point Paul listed his resume of the things that he had endured to be able to boast if he wanted to. Check Paul out:

2 Corinthians 11:24-26

24*Five times I received from the Jews the forty lashes minus one.* **25***Three times I was beaten with rods, once I was stoned, three times I was shipwrecked. I spent a night and a day in the open sea.* **26***In my frequent journeys, I have been in danger from rivers and from bandits, in danger from my countrymen and from the Gentiles, in danger in the city and in the country, in danger on the sea and among false brothers,*

If we are not willing to endure certain things, just like Paul, for the good of the Kingdom, then we will never finish this race. Praise God that most of us will not have to resist the kingdoms of this world to the point of giving our life, but we should have the same exact resolve to do so if that is what God needed.

Most of the terrorist activity in the U.S. in recent years has come not from Muslims, but from radical Christianists, white supremacists and far-right militia groups. So what would you do if someone walked into your church on a Sunday morning and said all Christians stand up? Hopefully you would stand up for Christ, however, many of you reading this book are shaking your head right now and saying no way.

If you have just said no way in your spirit, then you have just denied Christ in your spirit, and need to ask God for forgiveness. All of the disciples, later to become apostles, either gave their life, or almost gave their lives for the cause of Christ. They all had finisher's grace and therefore, they all received the Crown of Righteousness that Paul was referring to in 2 Timothy chapter 4.

Why is this so important? Because God is looking at our hearts and the more Christ like we become the more complete we become. Not only in God but in every area of our lives. If you know that your life is not your own but it's God's to wield as He will, then how can you be habitually depressed? How can you live in lust? How can you live in anger? Can you really afford not to forgive?

Of course the answers to all of the aforementioned questions should be no, but we know that in reality we don't always answer this question correctly. Finishing grace requires beginning faith. If you don't have faith in the abilities and promises of God you will never last past the pitfalls, detours, and hard times of life. Remember without faith it is impossible to please God.

Kingdom life is a marathon not a sprint. And so when we see someone that ran his or her race well we should definitely have a conversation with them to find out their secret.

Look at Paul, he himself said that he ran his race and fought the good fight of faith. Paul ran "the race" so well that he was able to encourage others. It was Paul that had to encourage and remind Timothy to not forget the laying on of hands by the elders that he received prior. And he also had to tell him to not let anyone despise him for his youth. When Timothy was ready to give up, he told him to preach the Word in season and out of season.

It doesn't matter what is going on in your life, you have to continue on. It doesn't matter who turns against you, just remember that God has not left you. Even when your mother or father forsake you, I'm here to tell you that God will lift you up.

When a person is running a marathon they start out with a host of people, after a while they either pull away of fall behind the pack. Either way there is always a time when you will look around and realize that you are running the race alone. It's at this point when the race transfers from being physical to mental, because your mind will just tell you to stop. Your mind will start asking you questions that make a lot of sense. Like for example, "Why are you doing this? Just stop." A marathon runner is trained to ignore these quitting impulses and voices and keep on pushing.

Likewise, we have to train ourselves when it seems like we're on our own and people are ahead of us to keep on running. Keep on living. Keep on believing. And keep on fighting. Because the race is not given to the swift but to those who endure to the end.

Any professional athlete will tell you that the mastery of their respective bodies in whatever sport or discipline that they're in, is 90% mental and only 10% physical. The body will do whatever the mind tells it to do, so we have to have strengthen our mental state in order to really achieve true strength.

Our command of the scriptures and our walk with God is very similar to the Olympic and/or professional athlete. We have to tell our body that we can do all things through Christ who strengthens us and that losing is not even an option. Our mental state which we could argue is the seat of our soul, meaning our intellect, personality, and the such is more important than anything going on physically because we have to be self-disciplined, which is all mental, to maintain our bodies as a living sacrifice, holy, and acceptable unto the Lord our Savior.

Once we discipline the mind we can then discipline the body. I am reminded of another saying of Paul when he said that he beats his body into subjection. We must do the same. God give us a finisher's grace!

1 Corinthians 9:24-27

24 *Do you not know that in a race all the runners run, but only*
one gets the prize? Run in such a way as to get the prize.
25 *Everyone who competes in the games goes into strict*
training. They do it to get a crown that will not last, but we
do it to get a crown that will last forever. 26 *Therefore I do*
not run like someone running aimlessly; I do not fight like a
boxer beating the air. 27 *No, I strike a blow to my body and*
make it my slave so that after I have preached to others, I
myself will not be disqualified for the prize.

CHAPTER 10

DWELLING IN HIS FULLNESS

Colossians 2:8-10

[8] *Beware lest any man spoil you through philosophy and*
vain deceit, following the tradition of men according to the
rudiments of the world, and not in accordance with Christ.
[9] *For in Him dwelleth all the fullness of the Godhead*
bodily.
[10] *And ye are complete in Him, who is the head of all*
principality and power,

An incomplete and incorrect view of God will transfer

into you having and incomplete life. It will sometimes lead to you living an incorrect life. The more accurately the eyes of your spirit see God the more impact He in His divinity and power has on you.

Just as in the natural the more you gaze into the Sun the more you can't see anything else, and would probably damage your natural eyes, but it's the same way in the spirit realm. The more that you look on the Sun, the more you can't see anything else.

When we're looking through the lens of the flesh all we can see is what the flesh is capable of viewing. For example, when you look at yourself, what do you see? Most likely you see someone who is imperfect and lacking in many areas. Very few of us if we're brutally honest, looking at ourselves, will see ourselves as whole and complete in Christ.

The good news is that God does not see us in the way that man sees us. Man sees the flesh. God sees the spirit. God sees us already whole and complete in Christ. In spite of our imperfections, He sees us as new creatures, new creations, partakers of His divine nature and more than conquerors over our faults. And what He really desires of us is for us to see ourselves in the way that He sees us.

The scriptures let us know that all of the Godhead dwells within Christ bodily.

Colossians 2:9

[9]*For in Him dwelleth all the fullness of the Godhead bodily.*

Which means that the more that we abide in Him, the more He abides in us hence, the more complete we become. We worship one God, not three and as we keep looking at the Son, the brightness of His majesty fills our spirits and settle the matter in our soul regarding who Christ is. The more Son we get, the more peace is poured into our spirits and subsequently, our soul.

What we think we need or are lacking in, whether it is godly character traits or physical health, we already have in Christ. It's not that you are going to be complete in Christ someday in the far future, God just wanted me to tell you that you are already complete in Christ. And all that remains for you to accomplish, is to dwell in the fullness of Christ and walk daily in that completeness by believing that your completeness is true. Guess what?

Whatever you need right now, it is contained in Jesus.

Whatever you desire right now, it is contained in Jesus. Whatever you need, as long as you connect Him to it, is complete in Him. He is your complete healer, complete provider, complete forgiveness, complete righteousness, complete favor and complete protection.

So don't focus on what you don't have right now. Focus instead on how in Christ, you are complete in everything right now at this very moment. Instead of poverty, infirmity, weaknesses, lack, and defects, you will see His love, strength, wholeness, soundness, and completeness manifesting in you.

What is important in your life? Is it the immediate gratifications offered by this world? Is it the things that you possess? Is it the accomplishments that you have achieved? If these are the most important things in your life, I just want to inform you that you will most likely not see or hear from God as much as you'd like. Because God is not contained in our selfish ambitions even though He cares about it all. Understand that God's ways our higher than our way and His thoughts are higher than our thoughts and we have to raise our way of thinking and we have to raise our way of living.

Comparatively, let us do another form of self-inventory. What in your life demands most of your time, effort, thought and finance? An objective and honest answer to this may reveal what you really worship. Mental assent is worship. Whatever or whoever you give most or all of your mental proclivities too is in fact an idol in your life. Whatever or whoever we spend the most of our money on is in fact an idol. These things are our objects of worship if they are in a higher place than God in our lives.

If the things we prioritize are out of alignment with where our priorities are supposed to be, we will find ourselves in lack and we cannot expect to incur any of the true blessings of God in our lives.

Three characteristics of a Godly man or woman is humility, spirituality, and faith. When you have truly been touched by God there is a humility that is necessary to receive from Him.

One time, Jesus told a parable about a wedding in Luke 14:7-11. Let's look at it real fast:

Luke 14:7-11

7 *And He put forth a parable to those who were bidden, when He marked how they chose out the chief places, saying unto them,*

8 *"When thou art bidden by any man to a wedding, sit not down in the highest place, lest a more honorable man than thou be bidden by him,*

9 *and he that bade thee and him come and say to thee, 'Give this man thy place,' and thou begin with shame to take the lowest place.*

10 *But when thou art bidden, go and sit down in the lowest place, that when he that bade thee cometh, he may say unto thee, 'Friend, go up higher.' Then shalt thou have honor in the presence of them that sit at meat with thee.*

11 *For whosoever exalteth himself shall be abased, and he that humbleth himself shall be exalted."*

He was talking to a group of religious leaders called Pharisees. These Pharisees were convinced that they were God's gift to mankind. They did everything right, from the lens of the religious, that is. For example, they tithed, went to temple, helped the poor, and followed the law to the letter. Outwardly, they were really good. Inwardly, not so much. They lacked the one thing that kept them from truly following God; humility.

Humility is a missing virtue in much of our religious expression. Our nature, and our culture, tell us that we must become great and respected by others. However, this is incorrect in the eyes of Heaven. Because Jesus was teaching them to not to think of themselves too highly. For example, like we just read in Luke14, He told them to not invite themselves to the front of the room when you're invited somewhere. You should wait for someone to invite you to the front. That's humility. Too many of us think that we are entitled to places of honor, when in reality, we should wait to be acknowledged or summoned.

God will summon you to the front dear one, when you wait on Him patiently, with the right attitude. The attitude of the person that thinks that it is okay just to sit in the VIP seats without being told that it is for them, was the attitude that the people had in Luke, chapter 14, and I believe this amused Jesus. Are you amusing to Jesus? Or are you humble?

We are taught that true value is in people recognizing us, and seeing how wonderful we really are. Although pride is listed as a vice in the Bible, many Christians wear it as a badge of honor. We just want people to see our position, and praise us for our piety. If someone has to say something about your piety for you to feel complete, you are really the opposite of being pious, you are prideful.

Our spirituality is revealed by our actions and decisions. Spirituality is not religiosity. It's not how many services you go to or bishops and apostles you know. Spirituality is contained in your relationship with God. Does everything in your life point back to God? It should, because as we look upon the things in the natural we have to remember that it had to first be allowed in the spirit realm. Your spirituality will lead to a faithful prayer life and make you want to be around people with similar faith.

Which leads to the last component of a truly Godly person; faith. Without faith it is impossible to please God and so our faith should be inserted into everything that we go through in life. Faith is the substance of things hoped for and the evidence of things not seen and so our faith is an invisible component of our tangible life and without it we're doomed to fail.

It took faith for me to believe that the hurt that I lived

with for so many years would one day diminish. It took faith for me to understand that my weeping would only endure for the night, because joy was coming in the morning. It takes faith dear one to understand that even though you might be feeling empty right now that God will fill every void.

The Word is true dear one, but it is your faith that is going to activate it for you. Faith without works is dead. Hearing without implementing what you've heard is pointless. Trust every word that has been spoken over your life men and women of God and live a full life; a life where you're lacking no good thing, full and complete in Jesus Christ.

I'll be praying for you all. Love you all and even more important than my love, remember that God loves you. God bless.

ABOUT THE AUTHOR

Minister Sandra Black is a woman that is sold out for the Lord, her desire is to be used by God in any capacity that He desires.

If you desire prayer or to have her as a guest speaker.

Please contact her at ministersandrablack2691@gmail.com or visit her website at **https://www.bcocprayerline.org/**

www.ingramcontent.com/pod-product-compliance
Lightning Source LLC
Chambersburg PA
CBHW072201090426
42740CB00012B/2349
* 9 7 8 0 9 9 8 4 6 6 5 3 8 *